Dawn of the
Bunny Suicides

Dawn of the Bunny Suicides

Andy Riley

ANDY RILEY IS THE AUTHOR/ARTIST OF:

THE BOOK OF BUNNY SUICIDES, RETURN OF THE BUNNY SUICIDES, GREAT LIES TO TELL SMALL KIDS, LOADS MORE LIES TO TELL SMALL KIDS, SELFISH PIGS, D.I.Y. DENTISTRY (AND OTHER ALARMING INVENTIONS), THE BUMPER BOOK OF BUNNY SUICIDES, WINE MAKES MUMMY CLEVER AND BEER MAKES DADDY STRONG. ROASTED, HIS STRIP IN THE OBSERVER MAGAZINE, IS COLLECTED AS A HODDER & STOUGHTON HARDBACK.

HIS SCRIPTWRITING WORK INCLUDES BLACK BOOKS, THE GREAT OUTDOORS, HYPERDRIVE, LITTLE BRITAIN, THE ARMSTRONG & MILLER SHOW, THE ARMANDO IANNUCCI SHOWS, COME FLY WITH ME, THE 99p CHALLENGE, BIG TRAIN, THE FRIDAY NIGHT ARMISTICE, SPITTING IMAGE, SMACK THE PONY, GNOMEO AND JULIET, SO GRAHAM NORTON, HARRY AND PAUL, SLACKER CATS AND THE BAFTA-WINNING ANIMATION ROBBIE THE REINDEER.

LOOK OUT FOR NEW CARTOONS AT:
misterandyriley.com

ON TWITTER:
@andyrileyish

WITH THANKS TO:

POLLY FABER, GORDON WISE, CAMILLA HORNBY,
LISA HIGHTON & ALL AT HODDER AND
STOUGHTON, KEVIN CECIL,
ARTHUR MATHEWS AND ELLIOTT MILLER

FIRST PUBLISHED IN GREAT BRITAIN IN 2010 BY HODDER AND STOUGHTON
AN HACHETTE UK COMPANY

FIRST PUBLISHED IN PAPERBACK IN 2011

COPYRIGHT © 2010 BY ANDY RILEY

A CIP CATALOGUE RECORD FOR THIS TITLE IS AVAILABLE FROM THE BRITISH LIBRARY

ISBN 978 1444 71134 9

PRINTED & BOUND IN ITALY BY L.E.G.O. SPA. HODDER & STOUGHTON POLICY
IS TO USE PAPERS THAT ARE NATURAL, RENEWABLE AND RECYCLABLE
PRODUCTS AND MADE FROM WOOD GROWN IN SUSTAINABLE FORESTS. THE
LOGGING AND MANUFACTURING PROCESSES ARE EXPECTED TO CONFORM
TO THE ENVIRONMENTAL REGULATIONS OF THE COUNTRY OF ORIGIN.

HODDER & STOUGHTON LTD.
338 EUSTON ROAD
LONDON NW1 3BH
WWW.HODDER.CO.UK

FOR
BILL & EDDIE

HOLE
1

HOLE
1

TOY TESTING
DEPT.

FRESHLY
SQUEEZED
ORANGE
JUICE